The Fire

That Burned Me

Blessitt Johnson

The Fire That Burned Me.

The Fire That Burned Me.

I dedicate this book to those who have gone through narcissistic abuse and are now healing.
-Blessitt -

You are stronger than you think!

The Fire That Burned Me.

Books By The Author:

The Fire That Burned Me.

Contents

Part 1 

(The Attacks Of The Narcissist)

Part 2 🔥

(The Exodus Of The Empath)

The Fire That Burned Me.

" Play with fire and will you get burned …I
REPEAT!!! Play with fire and will you get burned
…"

Part 1

(The Attacks Of The Narcissist)

Narcissist

You took the best of me, paraded it and used my
emotions as a promotion
to display your ego but we'll see who gets the last
laugh.

Takers

They take but never give.

They use but don't choose.

They break but still fake behind a smile.

A **false perception** and a **false personality.**

Mask Wearing

Like a masquerade ball, you show up wearing one
of your masks to disguise yourself from me.
A part of me felt like this was a play and you were
rehearsing your lines.
Making sure you got your story straight before
making a grand entrance.
So you display your **facade**.

The Facade

What I perceived you to be is who I thought you were but realized it was just your facade.

You blinded me with your crisp words and luscious lips.

So I could not notice the abuse….

Fell in love with your words instead of paying attention to your actions.

So your **love bombs** felt like sweet kisses to my soul.

Love Bombs

The way you pretended to love me had me on cloud nine not knowing that you were preparing to finish me off.

Every touch of your soft but tender hands made me feel on top of the world until it was on top of me.

Suddenly your love turned cold and left me wondering why.

Days turned into weeks and weeks into months questioning if I ever existed to you.

You **discarded me** without warning and left me cold and dry…

Discard

I craved your attention and begged for your love but all I got was nothing…

Left without a trace and acted as if I wasn't alive in your presence which made me cold.

Threw me away like trash and tossed me in the dumpster until you were ready to dive for me.

Even then you handed me breadcrumbs of your affection.

crumb after crumb…

Breadcrumber

One day you care, the next day you don't.

One day I existed, the next day I did not.

Something I couldn't understand.

You showered me with love just to take me high

only to knock me down...

Gave me enough attention to ignite the hope of

things working out.

Only to kill it.

Making me feel like I wasn't enough.

But yet I still hoped you'd change...

Which opened the door to your **neglect**.

The Neglect

Used and abused.

Neglected and misconstrued.

I felt the weight of the mental bruises you gave and

the stabbing pain of the emotional games you

played.

Soon my whole being was neglected.

My time...

Attention...

Heart...

And my mind…

Yet you did not care as you **discarded me** again.

With no intention of clearing things up.

No apology in sight.

Discard Times Two

You danced in the streets with those girls.

The ones that had no integrity while I sat at home

wondering what I did wrong.

Not knowing that I was blaming myself for nothing.

You were guilty and I was innocent, yet I became

the villain.

Threw your love affairs in my face.

Boasted with pride about your lack of loyalty or

awareness of your actions.

I mentally planned my escape one day at a time...

Suddenly you noticed and sprinkled me with **fake

love**.

Fake Love

A part of me questioned why I stayed though my
heart yearned to leave.
Your weird behavior and soft gestures made me feel
like I was being pranked.
The deceptive compliments and flirtatious
demeanor took me for a spin in my head…
But I knew it was too good to be true.

I planned to find another love …
One that was real but fear overtook me.
Your **jealousy** rained and your **insecurities** ran
rampant at the thought of another having me…

So you spiraled in anger.

Insecure

In anger, you project your insecurities onto me causing me to crumble.

Making me feel insignificant just because you weren't enough.

Tried to trap me in your life so I could not escape.

 You played **mind games** by telling me I'll never find true love.

Guilt tripping me into staying by promising me a bunch of lies.

I surrender in defeat.

Sadly… I weep.

Mind Games

Manipulating my mind by making me believe that the words you spoke about me were true and that I needed to be changed.
Burning with regret of ever giving you another chance haunted me.
Here I was mentally drained inside.
You pour words of gasoline over my heart and let it burn without care.
Standing aside laughing at my heart as it turned black and blue.
These mind games were the starter to your **gaslighting.**
Something I could not bear.

Gaslighting

Like a lighter you lit my mind with accusations and conversations I did not know would burn.

Made me believe that the things you perceived were true and my view was skewed.

The **manipulation** and constant contemplation of throwing me away.

Killed me...

I burned even more.

The fires you set left me with only ashes to eat.

Manipulation

Your obsessive control pained me and your refusal
to take accountability flustered me.
So I choose to expose your behavior, only to be
confused in the end.
Shifting blame so that you don't seem like the
villain made me feel **boxed in by your lies.**

Don't Box Me In

Who I was, wasn't enough to keep you amused so
you slandered it.
Belittling me for who I am.
Just because you felt insignificant and small.
 You sought to bring me low.
Made me change who I was to fit in your box.
The false perception and flawed impressions you
had of me because you wanted to paint me as evil.
While you were the saint.
"Don't box me in,"
I screamed but you wouldn't listen.
So I lost **control…** drowning in tears.
Yelling at God to punish you for what you've done
to me.
Deliverance is what I craved.

Control

Who were you to tell me what to do and how to
live?
Who were you to think you were my master?
Your **obsessive control** is what stole the joy in me.
I seek to be released.

Obsession

You watch and creep.

I run, you peep.

Waiting for me to make a move.

Your obsession, like I'm your possession, has driven

me insane.

So I go **no contact** to survive.

Part 2

(The Exodus of the Empath)

No Contact

I cut the cords to communication
and boarded the walls to my vulnerability so you
could not sneak in.
I **cut** the ties to **access** and made my **absence
known**.
Making sure my healing would resume.

Physically Left

Days went by since communication was cut.
I prayed and I pleaded for the strength to physically
leave for good.
Because I knew you'd return to reel me in.
So I wiped my tears, laced my shoes, and walked
out quickly.
Opening the door to my healing and the end to your
deceit.

You notice…
And with anger, you **smear my name….**

Smear Wars

Painted my name around town like you were an
artist and spewed vile lies to butcher my character.
Smeared it from east to west so freely yet I stand
strong, internally hurting from this bruise of abuse.
Gliding your paint brush over people's heads
making them believe I was the abuser knowing
what you did.
So I learned that my side of the story didn't matter
and that God defends me.

I proceed to give **no response**.

A blank face with **blank emotions…**

No reaction at all.

No Reaction

While minding my business suddenly you seem to
find a way to access me.
Invading my space with your words of gentleness
I give no response.
So you proceed to get my attention by making your
presence known.
But I don't give in.
You puff up your chest and prance around making
yourself important as if it would impress me but
fail.

I stand looking in **silence**.

Purposely… **ignoring your show**.

Silence

Months go by and I begin to grow stronger with time.
Your efforts to appease me only made me wish I never knew you.

I continue to move in silence.

While you desperately wanted my attention like I begged for yours months ago but **failed to supply.**

So you try other tactics.

New Supply

Copy… paste… delete.

My energy was so authentic and my heart was so
genuine that it left you sprung.
Tried to move on but it ended before it started.
Hoping to find another me… another victim to
abuse so you plan to take what was close to me.
Leaving me questioning close friends.

In efforts to warn… I was swiftly interrupted by the
smell of her bitter competition and jealousy.
Not knowing she was in deep water.

So I continue to remain on mute.

Don't Spin The Block

Thriving in my life and healing from bloody wounds.
You cunningly crept into my life without permission.
After realizing I was doing better than ever without you.
You attempt to lift me off my feet as if I didn't see your true colors bloom.

Tugging at me as if I belonged to you and treating me like I was your **most precious possession**.
But the truth is I am not.

Not Your Possession

When did I become your prize?
Who told you that you were my owner?
A delusion you've set yourself in.
I am not your play toy nor am I your beneficial
accessory.

You don't own me.
I am not for sale nor keeps.
I say with confidence.

As **I see you** creeping from a distance.

I See You

Around the corner, you peep and in public places,
you creep up watching me from afar.
Awkwardly making yourself invisible but I see you
creeping.
Sneaking into my bubble just to bring in my
presence and recognize what you've lost.

I see you lurking in the distance so **I use
discernment**.

I watch your every move.

Discernment

Stop playing and start thinking about ways to keep you away.
I aimed to flourish, all while beating you at your own game.
Discerning every move.
Alert and awake to your levels of attack.
Soon life went **mute** and **quietness became my friend.**

The Beauty Of Quietness

The soft sound of a pin drop and the sweet aroma of
silence filled my soul.
This beautiful sight of living in solitude made me
fall in love with the depths of quietness.
It gave me a sense of hope and patience.
So I treasured it effortlessly.

A beautiful picture of what **stillness** looked like and
what made my life complete.

Costly peace.

Costly But At Peace

Breaking free cost me everything.
My heart.
My friend's.
My reputation …and character but it was worth the
peace I found.

When I thought I had lost my mind God made sure
that peace rested on me when things got rough.
So the **rhythms of freedom flowed easily.**

Sounds of Freedom

The flow of its song made me dance and the rhythm
of its beat soothed my soul.
I was finally free.
Free from the hurt.
Free from the abuse.
Free from betrayal.
Free indeed.
So I groove down streets to **remember who I am**.

Know Who You Are

Being with You made me forget who I was so I leached off of who You were hoping to find my identity again.
But quickly figured out this was wrong.
Now I have time to think.
He handed me my identity and showed me who I was so I would know who I am.

God whispered, " Know who you are."

I smile with glee.

It was the **strength** I needed to remain **strong**.

Stronger Than You Think

Never knew I could be this strong after you exposed
all my weaknesses as a way to make yourself
bigger.
In your eyes I was weak but I proved you wrong.
I am stronger than you think.
Powerful…
 Bold……
  Bright….

Worthy of more than this jaded love you display.

So I seek it.

Worthy Of It

All my life I questioned whether I was worthy of
true love from all the abuse I've endured.
But the truth is I'm worthy of it.
Love.
True love.
One that does not bruise
One that does not use but **protects at all costs**.

About The Author

The author, **Blessitt Johnson,** born in 1999 is a writer and poet.
As a small-town girl in the heart of east Texas, after countless attempts to pursue a college degree and wondering where her future would go. She trusted God and years later pursued her passion of writing poetry books for those who struggle with mental health such as anxiety, depression, and loneliness just like her. While showing others how God is in every situation and every circumstance.

She also enjoys writing books that discuss real-life issues such as abandonment, trauma, and abuse. Blessitt spends most of her time at home with family and friends, going to the park, and traveling. For more information about upcoming books, questions or concerns contact johnsonblessitt57@gmail.com

The Fire That Burned Me.